W9-BNV-603

Your Favorite Authors

DAV PiLKEY

by Kelli L. Hicks

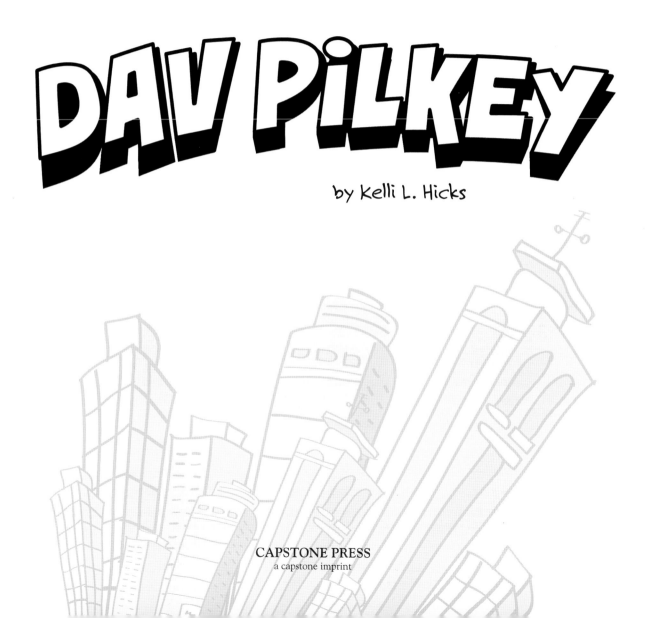

CAPSTONE PRESS
a capstone imprint

First Facts are published by Capstone Press,
1710 Roe Crest Drive, North Mankato, Minnesota 56003
www.capstonepub.com

Library of Congress Cataloging-in-Publication Data
Hicks, Kelli L.
   Dav Pilkey / by Kelli L. Hicks.
      pages cm.—(First Facts. Your Favorite Authors)
   Includes bibliographical references and index.
   Summary: "Presents the life and career of Dav Pilkey, including his childhood, education, and milestones as a best-selling children's author"—Provided by publisher.
   ISBN 978-1-4765-0221-2 (library binding)
   ISBN 978-1-4765-3436-7 (paperback)
   ISBN 978-1-4765-3418-3 (eBook PDF)
1. Pilkey, Dav, 1966–—Juvenile literature. 2. Authors, American—20th century—Biography—Juvenile literature. 3. Children's stories—Authorship—Juvenile literature. I. Title.
   PS3566.I51115Z65 2014
   813'.54—dc23
   [B]   2013003117

Editorial Credits
Christopher L. Harbo, editor; Tracy Davies McCabe and Gene Bentdahl, designers; Marcie Spence, media researcher; Kathy McColley, production specialist

Photo Credits
Alamy Images: Bob Daemmrich, 13, 15, 21, Bob Pardue – Signs, 5; Capstone: Michael Byers, cover, 19; Capstone Studio: Karon Dubke, 17; Courtesy of Scholastic Inc.: Karyn Baker, 9; Newscom: Ed Suba Jr./MCT, 11 (bottom); Shutterstock: Bedrin, 11 (top), Christopher Sista, 7 (bottom), lavitrei, design element, Rudy Balasko 7 (top)

Printed in the United States of America in North Mankato, Minnesota.
012015   008704R

Table of Contents

Chapter 1: A Great Start

When he was 20 years old, David "Dav" Pilkey entered a national writing and **illustrating** contest. His entry was titled *World War Won*. It told the story of a raccoon and a fox who struggle for peace. After a few months, Pilkey received an exciting phone call. He won! Even better, his story would be **published**. Pilkey's career as a children's author had begun.

---

illustrate—to draw pictures for books, magazines, and other publications

publish—to produce and distribute a book, magazine, or newspaper so that people can buy it

Dav

Dav's Name

Dav worked at Pizza Hut in high school. When he received his name tag, the "e" was missing at the end of "Dave." He liked the new spelling and became Dav (still pronounced like Dave).

Chapter 2: A Challenging Childhood

Dav Pilkey was born March 4, 1966, in Cleveland, Ohio. His dad was a steel salesman. His mom played organ at a nearby church. Dav grew up with an older sister. He went to elementary school in Elyria, Ohio. School was hard for Dav. He got bad grades. Teachers thought Dav was a troublemaker.

Cleveland, Ohio

BOOK REPORT

Dav's troubles in school were caused by **ADHD** and **dyslexia**. These problems made it hard for Dav to read and pay attention. When Dav bothered his classmates, his teachers made him sit in the hallway. To pass the time, he drew comic books. One character he created was Captain Underpants.

ADHD—short for attention deficit hyperactivity disorder; ADHD is a condition that causes people to have problems concentrating and sitting still

dyslexia—a learning disability that is usually marked by problems in reading, spelling, and writing

"When I was a kid making silly books out in the hall, I never dreamed that one day I'd be making silly books for a living."
—Dav Pilkey

Pilkey and his dog

High school was difficult for Dav too. No one believed his stories would take him anywhere in life. That all changed when Dav started college in 1984. One of his teachers at Kent State University encouraged him to write and draw. Then Dav won the contest with *World War Won*. He knew he should become a children's author.

Kent State University

Chapter 3: Successful Series

After *World War Won*, Pilkey worked hard to get his next book in print. *'Twas the Night Before Thanksgiving* was **rejected** 23 times before finally being published. Then he released *A Friend for Dragon* in 1991. This book about a blue dragon kicked off a successful five-book series.

---

reject—to refuse to accept something, such as an idea, drawing, or book

Sue Denim

Pilkey released *The Dumb Bunnies* in 1994. But he isn't listed as the author. Pilkey thought it would be fun to write the book using a fake name. He chose Sue Denim, because it sounds like the word "**pseudonym**."

---

pseudonym—a false name used by an author instead of his or her real name

Pilkey struck gold with *The Adventures of Captain Underpants* in 1997. In the book two fourth graders turn their principal into the superhero Captain Underpants. The book was a huge hit. Readers loved its silly humor and funny pranks. It sold millions of copies and led to nine more books in the series.

"Once kids discover that you can still be successful in life even if you're not successful in school, I think they'll develop more confidence and hope."—Dav Pilkey

Captain Underpants was so successful, Pilkey wrote several **spin-off** books. *The Adventures of Super Diaper Baby* was a huge hit. It reached number one on *The New York Times* best-seller list in 2002. In 2010 *The Adventures of Ook and Gluk: Kung-Fu Cavemen from the Future* became a best-seller.

---

spin-off—a book that features a character who had a popular but less important role in an earlier book

Pilkey has several successful series besides Captain Underpants. He released *Ricky Ricotta's Giant Robot* in 2000. Readers loved the story. But they didn't think the robot was actually a giant compared to the mouse. Pilkey changed the book's name to *Ricky Ricotta's Mighty Robot*. Since then Pilkey has released six more Ricky Ricotta books.

Awards

Pilkey has won awards for his books. *The Paperboy* earned Pilkey a Caldecott Honor Award. This award honors the best children's book artists every year. *Dog Breath: The Horrible Trouble with Hally Tosis* won the California Young Reader Medal.

"I was so surprised when *The Paperboy* won the Caldecott Honor Award. I can hardly even remember painting it. The only thing I recall is that I had to hurry up and finish it so I could start painting *Make Way for Dumb Bunnies*. I think I'm going to rush through all my books from now on!"—Dav Pilkey

Chapter 4: Dav's Secret

Dav Pilkey has written more than 40 books. Many of them have sold worldwide in 19 different languages. What's the secret to his success? Pilkey uses his creativity and **imagination**. He understands what kids like to read. Funny characters, silly jokes, and crazy adventures keep eager readers coming back for more.

---

imagination—the ability to form pictures in your mind of things that are not present or real

Personal Side

Pilkey married his wife, Sayuri, in 2005. They live near Seattle, Washington.

Pilkey with one of his fans

Timeline

1966	born March 4 in Cleveland, Ohio
1984	enters college at Kent State University
1986	wins The National Written and Illustrated by ... Awards Contest for Students
1987	*World War Won* is published
1997	*The Adventures of Captain Underpants* is published; Pilkey wins a Caldecott Honor Award for illustrations in *The Paperboy*
1998	wins the California Young Reader Medal for *Dog Breath: The Horrible Trouble with Hally Tosis*
2000	*Ricky Ricotta's Giant Robot* is published; the title changes to *Ricky Ricotta's Mighty Robot* in 2002
2002	*The Adventures of Super Diaper Baby* is published
2005	marries his wife, Sayuri
2010	*The Adventures of Ook and Gluk: Kung-Fu Cavemen from the Future* is published
2011	*Super Diaper Baby 2: The Invasion of the Potty Snatchers* is published
2012	*Captain Underpants and the Terrifying Return of Tippy Tinkletrousers* is published
2013	*Captain Underpants and the Revolting Revenge of the Radioactive Robo-Boxers* is published

Glossary

ADHD (AY-DEE-AYCH-DEE)—short for attention deficit hyperactivity disorder; ADHD is a condition that causes people to have problems concentrating and sitting still

dyslexia (dis-LEK-see-uh)—a learning disability that is usually marked by problems in reading, spelling, and writing

illustrate (IL-uh-strate)—to draw pictures for books, magazines, and other publications

imagination (i-mag-uh-NAY-shuhn)—the ability to form pictures in your mind of things that are not present or real

pseudonym (SOOD-uh-nim)—a false name used by an author instead of his or her real name

publish (PUHB-lish)—to produce and distribute a book, magazine, or newspaper so that people can buy it

reject (ri-JEKT)—to refuse to accept something, such as an idea, drawing, or book

spin-off (SPIN-off)—a book that features a character who had a popular but less important role in an earlier book

Read More

Fandel, Jennifer. *You Can Write Awesome Stories*. You Can Write. North Mankato, Minn.: Capstone Press, 2012.

Llanas, Sheila Griffin. *Picture Yourself Writing Fiction: Using Photos to Inspire Writing*. See It, Write It. Mankato, Minn.: Capstone Press, 2012.

Index

Internet Sites

FactHound offers a safe, fun way to find Internet sites related to this book. All of the sites on FactHound have been researched by our staff.

Here's all you do:

Visit *www.facthound.com*

Type in this code: 9781476502212

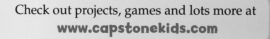

Check out projects, games and lots more at
www.capstonekids.com